A0487

D0437909

Date Due

JY 7 '89			
OC 29 '93			
MR 18 '94			
NO 16 '99			
AP 24 '00			
JY 22 '09			

QUICK
GUIDE
TO CHEESE

QUICK
GUIDE
TO CHEESE

How to buy cheese

How to keep cheese

How to serve cheese

How to select cheese

ROBERT JAY MISCH
DRAWINGS BY ROBERT PSOTTO

Doubleday & Company, Inc.
Garden City, New York

(With thanks to Stephen H. Speier of the Schratter Co., and Mary Lyon of Foods from France, for their help along the line. And to Phil Alpert of "Cheeses of All Nations," for starting me off as a turophile, many years ago.)

ISBN: 0-385-07446-8
Library of Congress Catalog Card Number 72–96249
Copyright © 1973 by Robert Jay Misch
All Rights Reserved
Printed in the United States of America
First Edition

CONTENTS

Dedicated to "GA"—
and to Sara, Emily, and Carolyn—
her three "Quick Guides" to the Nursery!

INTRODUCTION

"Cheese it!" That was my earliest recollection of the word "cheese"! It meant "Watch out—duck it—it's the teacher" or "Shh! Mom's coming up the stairs." I never did know why, any more than I understand why the term "a piece of cheese" should be the ultimate put-down. But today "Cheese it!" simply means that someone is suggesting a Sauce Mornay.

We all have some acquaintance with cheese. Usually it begins with a package of Philadelphia Cream—and all too often it ends there. But somebody must be doing something right because we produce several billion pounds every year and import additional quantities (nearly 140 million pounds last year) from all the other cheese-making nations. Some of us must be eating a lot of cheese. While we're not in the same league with such cheese consumers as the Italians, fifteen pounds per year per capita isn't bad. Half is from Wisconsin—the rest from New York, Vermont, and California, primarily, and a small portion is imported. Denmark is our leading exporter; then Italy, Switzerland, Holland, and France.

Even to this day, though, because of restrictions imposed by Uncle Sam and the American insistence on blandness and the *pretty look,* consumers of the imports are at least 65 per cent foreign born or first generation. As the Schratter people (one of the biggest and best importers) say, *"Les Américains mangent avec les yeux."*

1

What Is Cheese?

Our good old friend the Encyclopædia Britannica, in its unromantic way, says, "Cheese is a solidified preparation from milk, the essential constituent of which is the proteinous or nitrogenous substance 'casein.' All cheese contains in addition some proportion of fatty matter or butter, and in the more valuable varieties the butter present is often greater than the casein." What a way to describe the sensuous taste sensation of a Brie oozing creamy lusciousness, or of a crumbly, sharp-mild Colby, smelling of clover and grass and conjuring up pictures of hot apple pie. (Incidentally, the true "greening" of America is the one used in a proper apple pie!)

How Is Cheese Made?

In every country where milk is produced and there is excess over fluid needs, cheese is made. The making of every type of natural cheese is the same, with variations. It involves the separation of solids from liquids by the curdling reaction of lactic acid (for fresh cheese) or rennet (made from the stomach lining of animals) for all major ripened cheeses.

The reasons for the vast variations in the cheese lexicon are many:

The milk—is it from cows, sheep, goats—or, yes, asses, camels, mares, buffaloes, or reindeer? The breed of the cow plays its part. The season of the year and the pasturage condition all contribute. Whether it is pasteurized or isn't is a vital consideration.

The microorganisms in the milk and the atmosphere—these
are either naturally present or introduced by man. These
are the ripening agents. Gas-producing bacteria result in
the holes in Emmentaler (Swiss); when inoculated into
the interior, you have blue mold cheese (Roquefort); when
on the surface, Brie or Camembert.

Basically, the cheese maker, whether he be a peasant, a "cottage maker," or a factory, simply provides the conditions for
nature to do its work.

This is very much the same as in the case of the vintner. But
just as the vintner can do all manner of things before, during,
or after fermentation—heat or cool the must, ferment with the
grape skins or without, chaptalize or water, etc.—so the cheese
maker can vary the amount of rennet, the temperature of the
milk, the draining, molding, pressing, mulling, or cooking of the
curd, the time and place of ripening. Each variation results in
another cheese. As a matter of fact, simply changing the locale
and then proceeding to make cheese in an identical way will

often result in a different cheese. A Cabernet Sauvignon grape, by the same token, produces a different wine in Bordeaux than it does in the Napa Valley, though everything in the processing be the same.

Not to labor the wine analogy, it *is* apt and the only one that comes to mind in discussing cheese.

To some, wine is simply food, a requisite for the daily meal.

To others, the oenophiles, wine is a beverage of interest and infinite variety—collected, hoarded, aged. So with cheese. The true defenders of the faith are called turophiles.

To some, wine and cheese are simply the varieties made in their own locality.

To others, wine and cheese are the subject of world-wide search and eclectic in-gathering from the seven seas.

To some, the taste or smell of a wine or a cheese is, well, simply the taste or smell of wine or cheese.

To others, the savoring of the subtle nuances of flavor, the differentiations of the "nose," the appraisal of the colors, the judgment of the body or texture—all these are integral parts of the discriminating palate. They are the sophisticated rites of gastronomy—not only for the sybarite but even for just the normally sensitive and inquiring gourmet.

The History of Cheese

Every cheese pundit harks back to the legendary Arab who put some milk in his saddlebag, made from the stomach of an animal, and went galloping off across the desert. That night, he broached the bottle, to find the milk had separated into

liquid whey and solid curd. He slaked his thirst with the whey and appeased his hunger with the curd. He did not realize that the chemical reaction of the rennet in the stomach had performed its magic—coagulating the curd—and making the first cheese!

Legend or not, cheese as a food has been traced back to the Hittites of over nine thousand years before Christ (just as, for that matter, has wine). That it came from Asia is indisputable.

The Sumerians speak of it four thousand years before Christ, so we can assume that lovely Queen Nefertite may owe some of her beauty to the healthful qualities of cheese.

The Greeks honored Aristaeus, son of Apollo, as the giver of cheese.

But it is to the Romans that we must award the Oscar for the popularization and dissemination of cheese and cheese-making know-how and know-where. They started the making of cheese in Britain, spread it throughout Gaul, the Low Countries, Iberia. *Formos* is the word for the wicker baskets used to drain cheese. It becomes *forma* in Latin. *Formaggio* is the Italian; *fromage,* the French. *Caseus,* cheese, is also Latin, leading to *käse, kaas* (Dutch), *cais* (Gaelic), *queso* (Spanish), *cyse* (Anglo-Saxon), which later became cheese.

The Roman legions traveled on cheese just as cheese is a standard army ration today. It was an important food in the Middle Ages; the monks of many monasteries took up its manufacture. Unaccountably, it fell into disfavor during the Renaissance and Elizabethan days. There grew up a superstition that cheese made one ill. There is record, however, of cheese accompanying the Pilgrims to Plymouth Rock. Just as unaccountably, in the nineteenth century, cheese came back strong, regained its respectability, and was accepted once more as the healthful food that it is.

BUYING CHEESE

There is great joy in learning enough about cheese to buy with authority—knowing *what* you are getting and *why* you are getting it.

Stores

While there may be much to be said for the rural or small-town life, there is not, when it comes to buying cheese! Henry Thoreau may have adored his Walden, but there was no place for miles around where he could get a good Brie. Maybe that's why he said, "Men live lives of quiet desperation." Except for an exceptional gourmet shop or cheese store crying in the wilderness of the small town or city, or a roadside stand purveying local wares in Wisconsin or Vermont, your real turophile must look to the large city for an adequate selection of cheeses. A few supermarkets, featuring "delis," may have a few of the more popular imports, but for the most part the shopper is confronted with a quarry of packaged nuggets containing bits and pieces of processed cheeses and some natural ones such as Liederkranz

or Borden's Camembert. He will also find gift-wrapped wedges of Cheddar of varying degrees of sharpness, and, of course, hunks of Blue. But in the large city he can revel in the variety of the cheese specialty store, the delicacy department of the great department store, and the ethnic foreign shop, dispensing Italian or German or Scandinavian or French products of all types.

Sampling

The only reason for emphasizing this is that, unless you have such a store, where cheeses are in large sizes and from which pieces are cut, you can't avail yourself of the #1 privilege of the cheese buyer—to sample! But even tasting isn't simple. The great cheese impresario, Pierre Androuet, he of the famous Paris cheese restaurant, cautions us to "taste soft cheese by pressing it with the whole tongue but hard cheese you taste only with the tip!"

Choosing

Androuet wrote a now famous letter to his daughter (age fifteen). It is full of wonderful hints for the cheese buyer. He wants her to be "an accomplished woman of the house" and so he admonishes, "You don't have to know how cheeses are made—only how to choose cheese and how to present a harmonious cheese platter to your guests—*at least four!*"

Timing

He also brings up a vital point, timing—which, of course, is more practical in France, which has hundreds of cheeses to choose from, many of which are generally available in good restaurants and stores even in the smaller villages.

What Pierre Androuet means is to get to know the seasons of cheeses and buy them when "in season." In his own words, "Be guided by the dinner, the nature of the cheese, and the season of the year." For Androuet, fall is the best time for cheese, and summer the most difficult, especially for the soft cheeses.

Other Factors

Grass is one great factor, of course even your butter is yellower and richer when the cows are out to pasture—but Androuet goes further than vegetation. He recognizes that precipitation in the area, the climate, the type of soil, and the kind

9

of animals that produce the milk—not just cows vs. goats vs. sheep, but what breed—all make a difference.

Hints from Androuet

Here are a few of this cheese pundit's greatest bits of advice:

Choose your store well. Is there good variety? Are the cheeses kept separated so they don't become too friendly with one another and share flavors? Are they kept separate from hams and bolognas for the same reason?

Be eclectic—serve many varieties—try new ones—vary your textures on the same cheese platter—vary your strengths so there'll be a cheese to everyone's liking.

A few specifics—don't freeze Roquefort. Brie and Camembert are no good for a picnic—they don't travel well in a car. And finally, the Frenchman comes out in the end—don't eat Brie or Camembert too *"coulant,"* or runny, because it's *"pas écono-*

mique." He's right, of course. These cheeses, when they run all over the plate, are not *economical*—but *I* love 'em that way! So there.

But I'm right back in his corner when he ends up by writing, "I would say to a son ready to marry my Colette—Pity the poor girl who has not in her life learned to know love, wine, truffles, music—and cheese!"

SERVING CHEESE

Temperature

In my opinion the one overriding essential is a decent temperature: 50° F. to 55° F. is about right for most cheeses, but the normal refrigerator is colder than that, and cheeses, emerging, resemble Eskimo Pies. That may be all right for ice cream, but it isn't for cheese. If you must use the refrigerator, choose the warmest part. The freezer compartment I'd leave strictly alone, though Swiss and Provolone don't seem to suffer much. Brick, Cheddar, Edam, Gouda, Münster—even Camembert—are successfully frozen, but do it fast and do it low (0° F.). The main thing is not to keep switching temperatures—cold, hot, cold again, etc. Again I revert to the analogy of wine—wine doesn't like frequent switches either. One constant temperature, even if it's not optimum, won't do great harm. It's the taking out and putting back that cheeses (and wine) object to. Keep the original wrappings on when possible. Cover cut edges with foil or wax paper or Saran wrap.

Another thing—this too like wine, *red* wine, that is—serve cheese at room temperature. So you'll have to take the cheese from the cooler an hour or two before dinner and just let it sit.

You're not the only one who serves his cheese too cold. Even so austere a magnificence as the French Line served hard-as-a-rock cheese the first meal out. I asked to have *my* Brie, Camembert, and Pont l'Évêque removed from the cooler and kept on a side table for me during the voyage. They were. The cheeses were perfect and, even the last day out, didn't cause notable discomfort to the sensibilities of other passengers.

Bread and Butter

Bread and butter go with cheese—French or Italian bread with the milder ones; rye, pumpernickel, black bread, and such with the sturdier. Crackers—well, only a few. The English water biscuits (Carr's and Jacob's especially) do rather well, but those sweetish, short-bread types they pack with their "Crackers for Cheese" confound me. For sweet Gjetost maybe, but for what else?

Butter—yes, some people like it. I find it too much—butter *and* a rich cheese.

When?

When to serve cheese is another variable. There is the school that serves it *after* the dessert. There is the school that serves it with the salad. *My* school is the one that serves it after the entrée and before the dessert. It seems to taste better then. It's not competing with salad dressing. It's not fighting against the sweetness of the dessert. The exception I'd make would be if the dessert is fresh fruit. Then cheese belongs with it. I don't happen to like cheese before the meal with drinks—purely personal.

Do's and Don'ts

Do serve your cheeses on a nice cheese board—ample in size so there's no overlap. Or one of those marble slabs is excellent. It may be a bit overmuch to have a separate knife for each cheese, but certainly Brie or any delicate cheese should have its own.

Don't remove the rinds from Brie or Camembert—best part. Do remove the rind from wheels of Cheddar, or at least of that part which will be eaten at one sitting—the wax and the cloth. Do start your cheeses by cutting out a wedge so people will know that they're meant to be eaten and not just looked at.

Keeping

When you return the cheeses to refrigeration (if there's some left), wrap the Cheddars and such hard types in a damp kitchen towel—the delicate ones in foil or Saran (the latter is especially good for goat cheese). Those bell-jar cheese keepers are pretty good. They let air in, they let smell out, and they protect the cheese from foreign odors. Molds on the surface won't hurt anybody—just scrape them off. But the best way is to have no cheese left. Buy only what you think you'll need—then go buy some more.

Variety

Above all, offer a variety to suit the tastes of your guests—certainly two or three—and keep varying. You'll never run out of kinds. You wouldn't serve leg of lamb every time to the same guests, would you? (We had a great aunt once who did!) But above all—serve cheese. For one thing, it helps to finish the wine in a blaze of camaraderie. Heed Brillat-Savarin, who made the oft-quoted remark, "A meal without cheese is like a woman who has lost an eye." I don't know if I care to be quite that extreme!

WHAT GOES
WITH WHAT?

That's always the big question because it hasn't any answer. Your own sense of taste should be number-one arbiter. Following charts or tables doesn't make great sense—at least not to me. I would say that the last of the wine I had with the entrée is the one I finish with the cheese—just as simple as that. When I'm told (seriously) that I should have gooseberry wine with my Caerphilly, then I know something's got to give, and it won't be me!

I don't like champagne with *any* cheese. I already mentioned I don't like cheese with drinks before a meal—and that goes for dips, too. (I'll be burned as a heretic and impaled on a toothpick.)

I think the fresh cheeses—cream, cottage, farmer's, and the like—need no wine—if you insist, make it rosé.

Soft cheeses like Brie and Camembert—best with red wine.

The rich, delicate double and triple crèmes—German Rhine or Moselle, Alsatian flowery whites, or a delicate Bordelaise Graves.

Hard cheeses, like Cantal, Cheddar, Edam—red or a dry white, or beer.

16

Goat cheeses—"little" wines of any color—Soave or Entre Deux Mers.

Blue and Roquefort—red (except Stilton—that takes Port).

Italian cheeses—red (except Bel Paese—a white Orvieto Secco or Soave will do nicely).

German cheeses—beer goes with almost all.

Swiss and Gruyère—dry white Aigle or Graves.

Fruit—any cheese, and a glass of luscious Sauternes or Barsac.

The Kinds of Cheese

The "fresh" or soft cheeses—those bland fellows without much backbone. U.S.A.—Cottage Cheese is the big one, consumed in frightening quantities by dieters. It comes plain or "creamed," and when it's whipped it becomes "Pot" Cheese.

Cream Cheese is another favorite of the retreat-from-flavor set. It is ubiquitous. It isn't exactly lip-smacking and needs a strong bread or cracker to give it git-up-and-go. Farmer Cheese, a pressed relative of Pot Cheese, varies from locality to locality. Rather sourish, it needs sour cream as its crutch.

Italy—Mozzarella. This soft, mild, wet sort of cheese really came of age thanks to the pizza revolution. The flavorings of pizzas are what give Mozzarella its primary character. Ricotta is not exactly a flavor powerhouse either. It is, however, smooth and creamy—and useful. It finds its Svengali in the pastas. Lasagne, cannelloni—even just plain noodles—give it a *raison d'être*. In Italy, they have another fresh cheese, and I have seen it here but not often. I refer to Stracchino. Tart and creamy, it makes an admirable butter substitute.

France—Winston Churchill once said, "A country that offers 325 varieties of cheese is not a governable country." Well, the French seem to manage, despite the fact that they have more

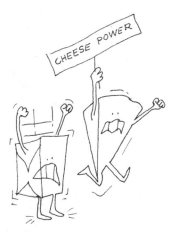

cheeses than all the rest of the world put together. A number are, of course, "fresh cheeses." Fromage Blanc is like our Pot Cheese. The French eat it with cream and sugar or make it into *coeur à la crème*. Demi-Sel is their cream cheese, but for real excitement one must turn to their outrageously rich double and triple crèmes. Petit-Suisse is a double crème. We usually get it frozen.

The Bland Cheeses. These are lovely cheeses but not block-busters. They are of the Bel Paese type—buttery and mild. The United States has its native Münster and Brick, and one called Gold-N-Rich, which isn't as bad as its name would indicate. Italy offers, besides Bel Paese, what I think is Italian cheese number one, Taleggio. And there is Fontina—excellent, especially the original Fontina d'Aosta. Holland's Edam and Gouda come in here, as the Danish Samsö and Tybo, France's Bonbel and true Münster, and German, Danish, or Norwegian Tilsit (Tilsiter).

Cheeses with Holes. Swiss—what sins are committed in thy name! If imitation is sincere flattery, then Swiss cheese must have the swelledest head in the world. Actually, true Swiss is Emmentaler and true Swiss has never been duplicated. Gruyère is both Swiss and French—from the two sides of the Jura. Both are excellent. Gruyère belongs in the fondue pot along with Emmentaler. Appenzell is the third member of the triumvirate but much less available, though you *can* find it. Raclette is special—it's the name used for the cheese used in this famous dish—although often it's called Bagnes. The cheese is put in front of the fire; as it melts, it is scraped and the semimelted scrapings are eaten at once. Sanen and Sbrinz are of this group though not generally available here.

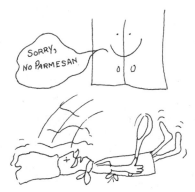

The Rock-Hard Cheeses. Parmesan is to spaghetti and/or veal cutlets as ham is to eggs—inseparable. Hard as stone, it is used for grating here (in Italy, and in some Italian delicatessens, it can be younger and softer, and a table cheese). Most of it comes ready grated in jars. It isn't as good as freshly grated Parmesan and you might as well face it. The real thing is called Parmigiano-Reggiano. A lesser-known variant is Grana Padano. Romano (or more properly Pecorino Romano) is usually seen grated and mixed with Parmesan. Without Parmesan, an Italian chef would simply quit. Switzerland has a rock-hard cheese too —Sapsago by name. It is pungent and greenish from the clover leaves added to it. It always comes in a cone shape. It takes plenty of elbow grease and a sharp grater to make it usable.

Cheddar, etc. The original Cheddar came from Cheddar Gorge in Somerset. It is antedated by Cheshire. Today Cheddar is a catchall for yellow, hard cheeses made in England, Europe, and certainly this country. Most of it is soap. A little Cheddar is still "farmhouse made" in England but isn't seen over here. But good factory-mades are available, especially from factories in Herkimer County, New York, from the co-operatives of Vermont, some from Wisconsin can be good, as is Tillamook from the West Coast; Canada does a good job, so does Italy, and France's Cantal, her most venerable cheese, can be super. Coon Cheddar, in its black rind, is exceptional, as is Colby from Vermont. California calls her entry Jack Cheese or Monterey Jack, though it is softer and really shouldn't be listed with Cheddars. Other Cheddar relatives include England's famed Double Gloucester (the "Single" stays home), Caerphilly from Wales, Scotch Dunlop; Leicester, Lancashire, Derby, and Yorkshire's Wensleydale. Warsawski is Poland's entry and Kasseri comes from Greece. Alas! poor Cheddar, I knew it well.

Incidentally, the U. S. Department of Agriculture gets into the Cheddar act. A "USDA" shield, reading "Quality approved," means the cheese has been inspected and approved for quality, as have the sanitary conditions under which it's made. A U. S. Grade "AA" shield is the highest quality, Grade "A' is also of good quality, though not quite as good.

The Filthy Rich! By that I don't mean dirty—I mean so rich in butter fat that there "ought to be a law." Double Cream has 60 per cent; Triple Cream, 75 per cent! Actually these cheeses are richer in butter fat than Brie or Camembert, which are rich enough. I refer to Crème Chantilly, "Monsieur," Triple Crème Parfait, Brillat-Savarin, Excelsior, and the "B" twins, Boursault and Boursin. These last two have become very popular, though personally I wish they'd left well enough alone and hadn't confused the issue with making these cheeses plain and also spiked with *fines herbes* and garlic. Very popular, these, with the cocktail set.

Brie and Camembert. These two, I think, deserve their own niche because they are two of the most popular cheeses in the world, two of the greatest, and two of the most difficult to get *"à point,"* or at the perfect peak of ripeness. They are ripened by bacteria and surface microorganisms. Both these cheeses are flat and thin so that the surface enzymes can do their job right through the cheese, which they couldn't if the cheeses were thicker.

These cheeses are copied extensively but rarely successfully. The true ones are made from unpasteurized milk, not available here, so that to taste these cheeses in France is an experience, whereas to taste them here is simply—well, highly pleasurable. American-made Camembert can be quite good though it isn't Camembert—more like a Carré de l'Est. Avoid, if you can, the ones cut into segments. No cheese can ripen properly once the rind is cut.

The same can be said of Brie. The foreign copies are seldom worth much, and that goes for the canned jobs, too. These may be cheese, but they're certainly not Camembert or Brie.

When these cheeses are underripe, there is a chalky midsection that refuses to do anything but stay chalky. If overripe, they both get ammoniated, smelly, and thoroughly unpleasant. To catch them at their few peak days is what the cheese hound delights to do—just as the wine man tries to drink his Claret at its absolute top. The only difference—the wine man has a few years, give or take, and the cheese man but a few days.

Carré de l'Est is a Camembert type and Coulommiers is a fresher Brie. Crema Dania is its own thing—a recent development and Denmark's proudest. It has the happy habit of ripening evenly and thoroughly.

The Blues. Even the veriest cheese tyro knows this family— the soapy-looking, off-white cheeses, shot through with blue mold. And that's what they taste like—mold.

Roquefort, the most famous, the most diligently protected, and the most expensive, owes its existence to three things: special ewe's milk, inoculation by a special penicilium made from rye bread crumbs, and ripening in nature's own drafty limestone caves of Roquefort-sur-Soulzon. Try, in buying, to get Roquefort that isn't too heavily salted for travel. While

Roquefort is unique, there are other good French blues. Bleu de Bresse is probably the best-known. It is softer by far than Roquefort—pastier, not crumbly. Auvergne, Jura, and Causses are others and Gex, if you can find it, is top drawer.

But Italy and England sport blue cheeses that are better known than these lesser ones of France. Gorgonzola from Italy and English Stilton are the worthies deserving of mention with Roquefort. The former is greenish rather than bluish, and it too is (or was) ripened in natural caves in the valley of the Po. It doesn't taste like Roquefort any more than it looks like it. Stilton is made around Huntingdonshire and Leicestershire from cow's milk and cream. It is not cave-ripened but matures without refrigeration. It is hard and crumbly when too young. Two things the makers deplore: the habit of spooning it out in bits and pieces from the top of a large cheese and pouring Port or Brandy into it. They say, cut it in pieces as you would any cheese. If it's not good, no amount of spirits *will* improve it; and if it is good, no amount of spirits *could* improve it.

There are other blues, but they shouldn't concern us much here. One, Blue Vinny, is worthy of note because, as André Simon, the great wine and food pundit, delighted to point out, it was rendered obsolete by English health laws, which forbade the making of it in barns where horses were kept. Under the resulting sanitary conditions, Blue Vinny simply wouldn't perform. It was discovered that the saddles and bridles harbored certain microorganisms that got into the milk and "Vinnied." No horse leather, no Vinny. I don't know what they're doing now, but Blue Vinny is once more available.

While such tales are interesting, they are not especially pertinent to us here, but the Scandinavian blue cheeses are. Danish Blue is today probably our most ubiquitous blue-veined cheese for two good reasons—it is good and it is less expensive. It is rich, dense, buttery, and very "blue." Norway, Sweden, and Finland also make blue cheeses, as do many other countries including this one. American Blue is pretty good but seems to me to have a bitterish aftertaste.

The "Holy" Cheeses. And I don't mean "holey," but rather cheeses that had their beginnings in monasteries or among the monkish.

Port-Salut, or Port-du-Salut, is the best known and came originally from the Abbey of Notre Dame de Port-du-Salut. It is basically quite mild and buttery but gets stronger with age—though never as strong as its Danish or American counterparts. St.-Paulin is almost identical with the French Port-Salut, Canadian Oka and German Tilsit. But by far the most important look-alikes is Pont l'Évêque from the Calvados area of Normandy. Stronger than Port-Salut, it is as hard to get *à point* as Brie or Camembert—over here, that is. All too often mine seems dried up, shriveled, and hard. It should be soft, golden, and sweet.

The Mountain Cheeses. Tomme (or Tome) means "cheese" in Alpine dialect. The most widely distributed is Tomme de Savoie from the Alps. It is not unlike a stronger Port-Salut. There are a number of other Tomes—Brach, Romans, etc.—

but only Beaumont is likely to come your way. It, too, is from the Alps. It has an orange rind and a pale flavor. St.-Nectaire is another—from Auvergne—not often seen here.

The Smelly Cheeses. Not that all cheeses can't be smelly —just leave any of them around too long, without refrigeration. But these cheeses are *meant* to be. Limburger, famous in song and story as the ultimate in stench, really isn't. Its taste is nowhere near as potent as its smell. Originally Belgian, it is now considered German, but most of ours is domestically produced. (There is a process Limburger—to be discussed further along.) If you were to ask ten people where Liederkranz is from, nine would hazard—Germany. Well, it's not and was originated in Upstate New York. It is probably our proudest original contribution to the cheese world (except perhaps for late-lamented Poona—no longer made, to my knowledge and distress). Liederkranz, reputedly the invention of a Borden chemist, took its name from Liederkranz Hall, a German club in New York (still extant). At its best—which it usually is, for Borden is careful and dependable—it is soft, glossy, honey-like in consistency. It should not be chalky (too young) or acrid (too old). Brick cheese is native to the heartland of America and is produced in Wisconsin. It is firmer than Liederkranz, holey and strong. Bierkäse or beer cheese, from Germany originally and now domestic, is very like it. Handkäse, or hand cheese (unlike the Hand melon, named after the Hand family), got its name because it was shaped by hand. The Pennsylvania Dutch like it, which is fine with me. The French, not to be outdone in anything, offer Livarot and Maroilles as their contributions to the stench of nations. Both are very good, once one gets over the aroma problem. Both come here in small quantities and both are worth trying.

The Cheeses of the Goat. I probably should not be writing of this category for, try as I will, I have still to acquire a real affection for "les Chèvres." I find most of them chalky, unyielding, except here and there such a one as St.-Marcellin. And I am wrong—no doubt of it—because your true cheese fancier often prefers them to the handiwork of the cow.

There are dozens upon dozens of goat cheeses, and they come in the cutest packages imaginable—tiny cylinders, ovals, pyramids, circles—for all the world like children's wooden blocks from Educational Playthings, the kind where you can only put *this* shape through *that* hole! Some are strong, some mild, some soft, most hard, some young, some mature (and, unless you're a zealot, beware those three- or four-month-old beauties —they sting the tongue).

Goat cheeses are mostly farmer-made because goats are unpredictable (if you scare 'em they don't give). And they're also inclined to be a bit on the expensive side because goats are that way and production isn't factoryized. But, for goodness sake, try all you can get hold of. They're fascinating. St.-Marcellin

in its chestnut leaf and raffia wrapping is adorable to look at, creamy and good. Le Banon is so steeped in Brandy you could get drunk. Valençay is around (often called Levroux), as is St.-Claude, sometimes marketed here as Claudel. If you want Crottin, you'll have to search, but look up its meaning before you do!

Aside from those of France, the best-known and much-beloved Feta is Greek made (or Balkan)—it's "sheepish" and some people love it. To me it tastes like brine. Provolone looks so great, but most of it really isn't. In Italy it was made from water-buffalo milk, which gave it its special flavor. Here it's usually from cow's milk but tastes like sheep. You can buy a whole one—from one to two hundred pounds!

Portugal is famous for good sheep cheeses—Queso de Serra is what you ask for. Pecorino Romano is the Italian sheep cheese you grate. The *dolce* is the sweeter one. The domestic comes already *grated* but isn't *great!*

The Novelty Cheeses (Natural). These are the cheeses that act as a culture for some foreign interloper—beneficial or otherwise. I will confess, at the outset, that I am a bit unreconstructed as far as cheese with additives is concerned, but I know I'm "square" that way and, I hope, fair as well.

Vermont sage cheese, for instance. I like it. It didn't originate in Vermont and the taste isn't really from sage, but it can be good—in moderation. It's English, actually, from Derbyshire, and a real sage tea was used to flavor it. Now it's mostly oil of sage and an auslander green is introduced.

Caraway is the most used additive—the familiar seeds seen in rye bread. They flavor bland cheeses, such as Münster, and make it something you can taste. Kümmelkäse is just what it sounds like—like Kümmel, the drink, which is also made from

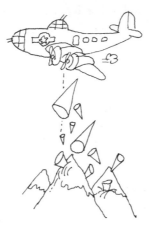

caraway. Nagel is one from the north lands flavored with cloves, and there's nothing reticent about cloves.

Gjetost is flavored with sugar, sometimes brown sugar. It's cooked. It tastes like diet chocolate. It's not my kettle of fish, but I love the Norwegians anyway.

Sapsago you'll always recognize. It comes in a cone, and if you drop it, it shatters the sidewalk. Dried clover gives it its color and aromatics. It's for grating. Manteca, or Manteche, is great fun, and I doubt if you'll find it except perhaps on Ninth Avenue, Manhattan, or in Little Italy. It's a Provolone (some say a Mozzarella) with butter squirreled into the interior, to wait your knife—meantime flavoring the cheese while the cheese returns the compliment.

Smoked cheese has become a new American "do." Everywhere, these days, you see those sausage rolls, or elongated blocks, with blackened rinds. They are sent as "gifts," which I know damns most things with faint praise.

Cheeses mixed with wine are more a type of spread than a specific cheese. Port mixed with Cheddar sometimes is a great favor to the Cheddar. Blue cheeses get the Sherry and Brandy treatment, with the same result. They're better than "dips," I think, but then I have admitted that this is a very personal book.

I suppose the new variations on Boursault and Boursin belong here, because now they're jazzed up with garlic, herbs, spices, and the like.

Liptauer is the end-all of flavored cheese. It's Hungarian. It's glop, until everything—and I mean everything—is added to it: peppers, paprika, capers or black olives, salt, sour milk, cream cheese, and so on. There is no *one* way to make Liptauer. There is no *one* way to get indigestion—but Liptauer will help.

Process Cheese. Can 50 per cent of Americans be wrong? I think so. That's the 50 per cent who purchase "processed" cheese, for 50 per cent of all the "cheese" we consume is processed—so it's either that 50 per cent consume it to the exclusion of all other, or else 100 per cent of us eat it 50 per cent of the time.

Process cheese suits the American mores to a T. It is mostly bland to the taste and easy on the palate. I remember writing an article, some years ago, about the great new popularity of the pale scotch whiskies that have swept the country. I called it "America's Retreat from Flavor." It applies just as well to cheese. That's why when one brave soul made process cheese from older, cheesier cheese and put it up against young, blander process, the latter won going away. Pity!

What is "process" cheese? Uncle Sam himself describes it as "A cheese made by grinding fine, and mixing together by heating and stirring, one or more cheeses of the same or two or more

varieties, together with an emulsifying agent, into a homogeneous, plastic mass . . . Lactic, citric, acetic or phosphoric acid or vinegar, a small amount of cream, water, salt, color, spices, or flavoring materials may be added." Cheddar accounts for great quantities but Swiss, Gruyère, Brick, Colby, Limburger, Blue, and others are processed. The cheeses are cut, ground, heated to 155°–160°, held there for three to five minutes—then packaged, and cooled. "It is practically sterile; it keeps well and does not ripen further." "Process blended" has cream cheese added and sometimes fruits, vegetables or meats. "Process cheese food" has milk, cream, or whey added. (The label *has* to tell you.) Those are Uncle Sam's definitions. Clifton Fadiman, with a little less restraint, calls it "the triumph of technology over conscience." I take my usual position—squarely on the fence.

Process cheeses have certain things to recommend them. They are economical. They don't require refrigeration until opened. They're easy to serve, to slice, to spread. They keep. They melt easily. They travel well. They're perfectly nutritious and wholesome. The only thing they haven't got is—flavor. (Except for the cold pack cheeses—Kaukanna, McClarens, etc.—which are combos of two or more natural cheeses, not heated.)

America is not unique today for "process." Scandinavia makes loads—so does Holland. Switzerland's process Gruyère is so prevalent as to confuse people who don't even know Gruyère au naturel. Italy makes some—process Bel Paese primarily.

Even France is succumbing. Strike me yellow if I didn't see Velveeta on sale at Fauchon. That's like finding "worry beads" at Tiffany! But after all, their own Gourmandise, Bonbel, even Boursin and Boursault, some say Vache Qui Rit—these, and others, are process.

But it's in America where process has reached full flower. Without Borden and Kraft, 50 per cent of the school children of America would die of malnutrition!

CHEESE
AND PASTEURIZATION

This is the process that makes mild men scream—and strong cheese mild. I shall tread gingerly.

The law says that unless a cheese is to be aged a minimum of sixty days, the milk used in its making (both here as well as for imports) must have been pasteurized. Those who feel pasteurization is a great deterrent to disease, point to outbreaks of typhoid during World War II attributable to nonpasteurized cheese. Contrary-minded, the cons point out the paucity of typhoid in all Europe, which eats cheese from nonpasteurized milk. They also gleefully direct our attention to the hundreds of thousands of vacationing American tourists who seem to weather the perils of nonpasteurized cheeses on their travels with equanimity. And then, rather waspishly, they deliver themselves of the opinion that the pasteurization requirement denigrates the flavor of imports and brings them down to a better competitive basis with the American made. You pays your money and you takes your choice!

CHEESE
FOR DIETERS?

Of course there are—plenty—but you have to be picky and choosy. You can't whip into those rich, gooey beauties—the Bries and Camemberts and the like—and expect them to be noncaloric! As that learned cheese man Eddie Edelman, of the Ideal Cheese Store, on Second Avenue, in New York, says, "You should go only by the butterfat." He points out that "Weight Watchers" try to eliminate water content, recommend-

ing only hard, dry cheeses. He doesn't agree—says it's only butterfat that makes a difference.

To minimize high butterfat, look for "made with [or partly with] skimmed milk" on the label. Also buy the "chèvres," or goat's milk cheeses—these are all about 15 to 17 per cent fat. Other cheeses for dieters include Reblochon, Pont l'Évêque, and St.-Paulin (France isn't big on dieting, you know). But Norway offers Jarlsberg, a kind of Emmentaler, which is quite acceptable, and Denmark has a coterie including Esrom, Tilsit, Tybo (Edam), Dambo (all part skim). Greek Feta and Italian Romano are within the pale, and of course Cottage, Pot, Farmer, and Ricotta are way down, with only 3 to 8 per cent. You *can* find salt-free and "part-skim" Cheddar, but you'll have to do a bit of scouting.

CHEESE
AND UNCLE SAM

There are wheels within wheels in every business, I suppose, but cheese seems to have more than its share. For instance, did you know that any cheese costing forty-seven cents a pound or less, F.O.B. Le Havre (beginning 1973, sixty-two cents a pound) must be *licensed* for importation into this country? Result the importers say to the French: "Please charge us more" so the licensing doesn't apply. *But,* and it's a big but, the result is you

can't have a good import at fifty-nine cents or seventy-nine cents a pound. You must pay eighty-nine cents or a dollar or more. You could, without these restrictions—which seem a little overprotectionist when you realize that all imports don't amount to much more than 5 or 6 per cent of the cheese we consume.

Take blue cheese. When it's "bleu" it's the imported; when it's "blue" it's domestic. This too is "on quota." Each importer is licensed for so many pounds. (The average is about three thousand pounds a year.) Here you can place some of the blame on the French, who, having their beloved Roquefort exempted from a quota, ask *us* to keep restrictions on all "bleu"!

But despite this in-fighting, demand for the foreign cheeses has increased 100 per cent in five years. The importers look at a 150–200 per cent increase over the next ten.

CHEESES, CHEESES AND MORE CHEESES

The following list is not by any means all inclusive. Some cheeses just aren't available. Some may be, but to such a limited extent as not to seem worth mentioning. Some—very few—may not be available here but are worth mentioning for your trip abroad. Some I know intimately; some casually; some hardly at all. The list, however, will serve to suggest how vast is the lexicon of cheese.

The list is alphabetical and includes cheeses of all nations, of all milks, and of all types. Where a cheese is something of an oddball, I shall not spend much time describing it. Even at that I shall try to abridge what could become a tome instead of a "quick guide."

Abertam (or Aber)—Czechoslovakia. A hard ewe's-milk cheese from Bohemia (near Carlsbad).

Alemtejo (or Queijo de Alemtejo)—Portugal. A soft cheese usually made from a combination of ewe's and goat's milk. Its prime claim to fame is that animal rennet is not used. The curding is done by using an extract made from

the flowers of a certain thistle—true of several other Portuguese cheeses.

Allgäuer Bergkäse (or Allgäuer Rundkäse or Allgäuer Emmentaler)—Germany. These cheeses are copies of the Swiss Emmentaler. Made in huge 150-pound wheels, they are, or were, so good that they used to be ordered by the carriage trade in Russia and aged in their cellars. There is also an Allgäuer Rahmkäse, which is soft and creamy, sometimes flavored with caraway.

Alpin (or Clérimbert)—France. As its name implies, from the Alps, not unlike the better-known Mont d'Or.

Altenburger—Germany. Goat cheese made near Thüringen.

American—U.S.A. An over-all name for Cheddar-type cheeses.

Ancien Impérial—France. Not unlike Neufchâtel. When fresh it is called Petit Carré and, when cured, Carré Affiné.

Appenzell (or Appenzeller)—Switzerland. Very similar to Swiss Emmentaler. Some is made from skim milk and some from whole milk. The latter is cured with the pomace or lees of wine and is milder than its commoner sister.

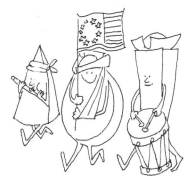

Appetitost (also Appetost)—Denmark. This is made from buttermilk. It is semisoft and quite tasty.

Armavir—U.S.S.R. Sheep's milk. Maybe we'll import some when that trade treaty is promulgated.

Asiago—Italy. One of the Grana-type cheeses—hard and granular. When two to nine months old, served at table, sliced. After nine months, hard, for grating. Some is made here.

Asin—Italy. This is a soft, dessert-type cheese usually eaten in summer and fall with fruit. After ripening for two or three months, Asin is known as Salmistra.

Backsteiner—Germany. Resembles American Brick cheese but tastes more like Limburger.

Bagnes—Switzerland (also Fromage à la Raclette). Very hard, it is put in front of the fire to melt and to be scraped onto bread that's "raclotto."

Baker's—U.S.A. A fresh cheese used to make cheesecake and other cheese pastries.

Banon—France. Of sheep's milk, in the Alps. It's a summer cheese, dipped in local Marc (a Brandy), and wrapped in chestnut leaves.

41

Barberey—France (also Fromages de Troyes). From the old Champagne area, a Camembert-like cheese, cured for winter consumption and sold fresh in summer.

Beaufort—France. A paste cheese, like a Swiss Gruyère but richer. Comes in big wheels, often with a few "eyes."

Beaumont—France. From the Savoy. Not unlike Trappist-made Tamié. Tastes somewhat like Port-Salut.

Bellelay (also Tête de Moine)—Switzerland. Another monastery cheese—soft and buttery, with blue veins. Long-lived. Not often seen far from Berne.

Bel Paese—Italy. In the world of cheeses, this is a relative newcomer—barely fifty years old! It is a soft, somewhat rubbery cheese. Bel Paese ("beautiful country") is a brand name of a number of local cheeses. Red Bel Paese is quick-curing, quite mild, and very popular. American imitations are made and sold under other names (Bel Paesino is one —no one would ever guess, would they?). True Bel Paese aficionados don't think they're nearly as good.

Bernarde—Italy. A cow's milk (90 per cent) and goat's milk (10 per cent) combination. A touch of saffron gives it the color.

Bitto—Italy. This cheese, from Northern Italy, is something like an Italian Swiss cheese. It can be made from cow's milk, ewe's milk, or goat's milk—or mixtures. When not fully cured (forty days or so), it is soft with large eyes. When made of skimmed milk and cured a year or more, it is so hard it is used for grating.

Bleu—France. These are the blue (or greenish) veined cheeses that everyone knows, led by that nonpareil, Roquefort. Roquefort is unique. Its name and method of making are jealously guarded, and it is the only bleu that isn't "licensed" by the United States; e.g., limited as to how many pounds per year each importer may bring in. Naturally, the Roquefort people like this special treatment very much. We shall have more to say about Roquefort under R. But under B we have plenty to occupy us. The great Androuet recognizes no less than eighteen *fromages bleus*. Some are only local, but many are well known and widely available. The principal cheeses of this marbled, flavorful group are

Bleu d'Auvergne—cow's milk, salty.

Bleu de Bresse—the famous name "Bresse," associated with transcendant chickens, has perhaps given the cheese an inflated reputation.

Bleu des Causses—from nearly Bordeaux. Aged in caves.

Bleu de Gex (also Gex and Haut-Jura), from the Jura. Cow's milk. Its mold is natural.

Bleu de Quercy—another cow's milk blue.

Bleu de Sassenage—cow's milk. Like Gex.

Blue—This large group of cheeses are made in many countries: the U.S.A., Argentina, Canada, Denmark, Finland, Sweden,

England. They vary in taste depending upon the milk used (cow or goat), the lactic starter used, the *Penicilium roqueforti* mold and its method of injection or natural induction, etc.

Danish Blue has arrogated a large share of the blue market. Blue Vinney (also Vinny and Blue Dorset) is hard to find. Once very popular, it became extinct because of new hygienic laws in England forbidding cheese-making in buildings where animals were kept. Without bridles and saddles, no microorganisms. Without microorganisms, no cheese! It is now being made again—scientifically.

Bonbel—France. A very popular, hard yellow process cheese of no great distinction.

Bondost—Sweden. A cow's milk cheese, originally farmer-made. Now factory-made in the U.S.A. and called Riks'ost or Bond Ost. With caraway added it's called Kommenost (Kuminost in Norway).

Boulette—France. There are a number: Boulette d'Avesnes, Boulette de Cambrai, Boulette de Thiérache. All are from cow's milk and hand-shaped.

Boursault—France. A relative newcomer that has really taken off in this country! A stand-in for Boursin (which see) if you prefer your cheese plain. Dessert cheese—75 per cent butterfat.

Boursin—France. A new "miracle" cheese that has caught on in the last three or four years. This very rich triple crème comes with herbs (and garlic), or completely encased in pepper. Popular as a cocktail cheese—much like the old "cream cheese and chives" dip.

Box—Germany. May be firm or soft, not unlike an American Brick in taste.

Bra—Italy. I like the name, so I include it, though I doubt you'll find much around. It's salty, hard, sharp, and almost chalk white.

Brick—U.S.A. A true native. Mild, with a sweetish flavor. Softer than Cheddar in body. Made in many states but mainly in Wisconsin.

Brie—France. "I think that I shall never see,
      A cheese as lovely as a Brie"

That poem is by me—my ode to, at least to me, *the* greatest cheese in the world. True Brie comes from the department of Seine-et-Marne. Melun, Coulommiers, and Meaux are most noted for the production of Brie. It is made in large and small flat discs with edible white crust and creamy yellow interior (when ripe)—chalky white when not. The mold on the surface finds its way inside to do the ripening. That's why the cheese must be flat and cannot be too thick. Winter is the best time for Brie. Rely on your cheese man to select a ripe Brie or one that will ripen for you when needed. Unripe Brie is a calamity, because then the cheese will not become *coulant,* or runny, the way Brie should be.

Brillat-Savarin—France. A relative newcomer, from Normandy. Semisoft, triple crème.

Bryordza (also Brinsen and Brinza). Hungary and Roumania. Sharp, biting, but creamy. Some is made in the U.S.A. When jazzed up with spices and other additives it is often called Liptauer.

Cabéçou—France (also Cabécon de Rocamadour). Gray-green golf balls of goat's milk.

Caciocavallo—Italy. A popular cow's milk cheese, akin to Provolone. Cured in pairs suspended by plaited straw strings.

Cured two to three months, soft, for table use. Cured six months to a year, hard, for cooking and grating. Taste is a cross between Gruyère-Cheddar-Provolone.

Caerphilly—Wales (Great Britain). Semisoft, cow's milk cheese. Comes in flat discs. Flesh is white and crumbly. Does not keep well.

Camembert—France. When good, it is one of the glories of France; when bad, it is horrid. The true came from Orne and migrated to Calvados (Normandy). A statue was put up to Mme. Marie Harel, who first made it in 1791. Much

copied all over France as well as in Denmark, Germany, and the U.S.A. Borden's famous "Military" version is *pas mal,* but it isn't true Camembert any more than Camembert is true Camembert even when made in the South of France. Like Brie, it should be soft and creamy, not hard or ammoniated, as it so often is. The crust is edible and delicious when *à point*, but not if it's wizened and dark brown and pulling away from the sides of the round box.

Cantal—France (also Fourme). This is a hard yellow cheese, usually seen in great big hunks. It is ubiquitous in France. It resembles Cheddar, though it is not as good as our best.

Caprice des Dieux—France. This little beauty is from the Champagne country. Know it by its oval box. Rich as all get out (60 per cent butterfat), it is happily being seen more and more.

Carré de l'Est—France. This one is from Alsace and Lorraine, and I find it not nearly well known enough. A soft paste cheese, it's delicate but with character. Not unlike Camembert. Sometimes cut in portions. As usual, I prefer the whole cheese.

Chantelle—U.S.A. An Illinois-made Port-Salut type. Quite sharp.

Chabichou—France. A soft, fresh goat cheese. April to December only.

Cheddar (also Colby and Jack)—English originally; now more American. It all began in the village of Cheddar in Somersetshire, so they say, but I opt for the true birthplace to be the cathedral city of Wells. It spread in colonial days to the colonies and then to upper New York, Vermont, and Wisconsin, which today account for the bulk of the tonnage—and huge tonnage it is.

Cheddar is hard, yellow-mild when young; orange, sharp when aged. Most (75 per cent) is made from pasteurized milk, in huge factories, though some is still "farmhouse" made, especially in England. The aging proceeds from three or four months to a year or even more. There is something beautiful about a crumbly sharp, well-aged Cheddar—something far removed from the stuff ordinarily called "store" cheese or "rat" cheese!

The best of the Cheddars go by such names as Coon and Herkimer County (both Upstate New York), Tillamook (Oregon), Vermont Cheddar, and Colby. Wisconsin makes the most, and some of it, when not sold too young, can be very good. The best Wisconsin is Longhorn. Also White Twin, Redskin, and Martha Washington deserve recognition. Colorado's "Blackie" is another contender for excellence, as is Nebraska's "Cornhusker." (Jack and Colby will be separately discussed, as they are not quite Cheddars.)

Cheshire—England (also Chester). The original feline mold gave the name to the "Cheshire Cat." It is more crumbly and open than Cheddar and doesn't age or last or ship as well. There are three kinds—Early Ripening made in early spring, Medium Ripening made in late spring, and Late Ripening made in summer. You'll seldom see any but the last.

Chèvre—An over-all name for goat cheeses.

Chiberta—A Basque country beauty. Flavorful and piquant, consistency of Bel Paese. It's lately available Stateside and well worth seeking out.

Christian IX—Denmark (also Kuminost). Usually contains caraway seed. Spicy.

Colby—A delectable Vermont cheese—a kissin'-cousin of Cheddar but moister and not as hard. One of our very best.

Comté—France (also Gruyère). A type of Gruyère. Some people like it better than the Swiss.

Coon—U.S.A. One of the very best Cheddars. From Upstate New York in a distinctive pitch-black rind and wax.

Cottage (also pot, schmierkäse, glumse, Dutch). A soft uncured cheese. It can be large- or small-grained. With only 4 per cent or more of fat it is "Creamed Cottage Cheese." Nutritious if not delicious.

Coulommiers—France. So much like a Brie that it is often called Brie. Delectable and widely *available*.

Cream—U.S.A. Soft, mild, uncured cheese not unlike the famed Neufchâtel and Crème Chantilly. Much used in cookery.

Crema Dania—Denmark (also Crema Danica). A relatively new arrival in cheesedom, and very welcome. A white, white soft-paste cheese with a dainty, luscious taste. Best of all it seems always *à point* and keeps well.

Crescenza—Italy (also Stracchino Crescenza and Crescenza Lombardi). Soft, creamy, fast-ripening, made September through April.

Creuse—France. A skim milk cheese. Aged in earthenware molds, it becomes dry and hard. Aged in closed containers lined with straw, it becomes soft and pungent.

Danablu—Denmark. The name for Danish Blue.

Danbo (**also Dambo**)—Denmark. Semihard, nutty, a type of Samsö.

Derby—England. A stand-in for Cheddar but not quite as good.

Domiati—Egypt. Soft, mild, salty—a "pickled" cheese—cured in salt brine. Sealed in tin for shipping.

Dorset—England (also Blue Vinney or Blue Dorset). A blue mold, white cheese. See Blue.

Dunlop—Scotland. Much resembles Cheddar, to which it is losing out.

Edam—Netherlands. Who doesn't know the famous red football? Not only is it exported all over the world, but it is copied all over the world. In Holland you will have Edam

(its sidekick Gouda) three meals a day. The reason, I think, is that the taste is flat, mild, not very demanding, and doesn't disturb anything else at the meal.

Egg—Finland. Whatever delightful little Finland offers us—from pottery to cheese, you can be sure it's different—and tasteful. Egg cheese is just what it sounds like. Eggs—aged eggs—are added to the curd. Rich? Phew!

Emiliano—Italy. A long-aged cheese (one to two years) usually used grated.

Emmentaler (also Emmenthal)—Switzerland. If you say "Swiss" more people will know what you're talking about! Emmentaler is the original, and the best, "Swiss" because it is made from "the milk of the Alps," which gives it that incomparable nutty flavor. It is made in huge wheels and aged six months to a year. Copies, of varying degrees of excellence, are made in all the Scandinavian countries including Finland. France (which does have "milk of the Alps") and Wisconsin make tons of it. Some of the latter, especially that made by the descendants of Swiss nationals, is not at all bad.

Epoisses—France. This is one of the prides of Burgundy—a semisoft cheese that has been laved in Marc (Brandy) of the Bourgogne and flavored with pepper, clove, or fennel.

Esrom—Denmark. A mild little cheese but with very marked flavor. Not unlike Port-Salut in color and texture.

Excelsior—France. A very rich, double-cream with 72 per cent butterfat. From Normandy. Not as well known as it should be.

Farm—U.S.A. (also Farmer). Usually eaten fresh by old ladies, who mix it (or buy it mixed) with sour cream, pepper, nuts, and fruits. Not unlike cottage cheese.

Feta—Greece (also Greek). Very soft and white, it is shipped in kegs containing milk. The taste is briny-milky-pickled. Much used for cookery.

Flotost—Norway. A cream cheese, much like Mysost.

Fontina—Italy (also Fontal). Both cheeses must be from the Val d'Aosta, Italy, by law, but copies are made in France, Sweden, Denmark, and the U.S.A. A cow's milk soft-paste cheese, but some is now made of ewe's milk.

Forez—France (also d'Ambert). If you like a cheese cured by burying in the dirt of the floor of a cellar, with water trickling over it, you'll like this one! I've not tasted it!

Formaggini—Italy. Name applied to a number of "small cheeses" of Lombardy, eaten at various stages of ripening.

Fromage à la Crème—France. The name of French cream cheeses—eaten while fresh: Franche-Comté, Morvan. (Coeur à la Crème is Morvan put into a heart-shaped mold.)

Fromage Fort—France. The name "Fort" (strong) is given to a number of "cooked" cheeses in the Ain Department and elsewhere in France. Most are mixed with berries, spices, and herbs and often with Brandy and wine.

Frühstück—Germany. A Limburger type—to eat at any time of day and at any meal from breakfast on.

Fynbo—Denmark. Firm, mild, aromatic. A "slicer."

Gammelost—Norway. A cheese for men, not boys. It is a semi-soft, blue-mold cheese with a sharp, aromatic taste that it gets from wet straw, two or three molds, and sometimes even juniper berries.

Gankasli—Germany and German-speaking Switzerland. The name given to soft cheeses made of goat's milk. Sold in small cylinders.

Garda—Italy. A soft, creamy cheese—edible crust. Comes in foil.

Géromé—France. A semihard cheese from the Vosges. Strong. (Sometimes with aniseed.)

Gervais—France. A cream cheese, like Neufchâtel. Comes in small foil-wrapped squares.

Gex—France. A bleu cheese from Ain, aged in caves. Resembles Roquefort. Good, too.

Gjetost—Norway. Formerly 100 per cent goat's milk (*gjet* is "goat" and *ost* is "cheese"). Today, mostly cow's milk with enough goat's added to keep the franchise. This is a cheese that takes no middle position. You either love it or hate it. Tastes a bit like a chocolaty fudge. Keeps forever—almost.

Gloucester—England. A hard cheese, between a Cheddar and a Cheshire. The Single is mild; the Double is mellow, and more emphatic.

Gold-N-Rich—U.S.A. Despite its name, a mighty good cheese.

Gomost—Norway. A soft, buttery cheese.

Gorgonzola—Italy. This is one of the world's great cheeses. It comes from Lombardy and Piedmont and is cured in Alpine cliffs. The white paste is shot through with greenish mold. It is creamy where Roquefort is crumbly. Of course it's been copied in many countries. We make a lot of Gorgonzola "type."

Gouda—Netherlands. This and Edam are Holland's most famous twins. A bit richer than Edam, it is strong without much bite. The Hollanders eat it for every meal, and in between. Copied in France, Belgium, Wisconsin, and Michigan.

Gourmandise—France. A processed cheese spread, flavored with Kirsch. Becoming very popular.

Gournay—France. A soft, fresh cheese somewhat like our cream.

Grana—Italy (also Parmesan, Reggiano and Padano). The name for a number of grating cheeses—granular and strong. Best known is Parmesan.

Grape—France. A buttery, mild cheese from the Alps. The rinds covered with grape pips.

Gruyère—Switzerland and France. Originally named for the storybook town of Gruyère in Switzerland. Made much like Emmentaler or Swiss, with smaller eyes—a bit creamier.

Hablé Crème Chantilly—Sweden. A superb cream cheese of fresh, delicate flavor, exclusive with one creamery.

Hand—Germany (also Harz Käse). Actually, I could just as easily attribute it to the farm families of German descent in Pennsylvania. Now factory-made and no longer really "hand." Germans like to melt it into beer, and *drink* it! It's sharp and pungent—very much an acquired taste. I haven't acquired it!

Havarti—Danish (also Danish Tilsit). Mild and bland, piquant aftertaste. Comes in aluminum foil.

Herrgard—Sweden (also Manor). A semihard cheese with a pleasant nutty flavor, akin to Emmentaler.

Herve—Belgium (also Hervé, which is wrong). Not unlike Limburger—soft and usually hopped up with herbs.

Holsteiner—Germany. A skim milk and buttermilk cheese.

Ilchester—England. A new cheese from Somersetshire, developed by chance by a man working on a new cream cheese. Said to contain beer.

Ilha—Portugal. A hard Cheddar-like cheese made in the Azores.

Incanestrato—Italy. A ewe's milk cheese from Sicily, bearing the imprint of the wicker basket molds in which it is made.

Jack—U.S.A. (also Monterey Jack). First made on farms in Monterey County, California. The cheese is made somewhat like a Colby. It is semisoft. When made of skim milk, it hardens and is used for grating. Very popular in California. (Sh-sh! I once had a piece of unpasteurized Jack—good, too.)

Jarlsberg—Norway. Not unlike Emmantaler, but not as "nutty." Low in fat.

Jochberg—Germany. Made from a mix of cow's and goat's milk in the Tyrol.

Jonchée—France. I've never tasted it, but I'd like to. It's flavored with rum, orange-flower water, and/or coffee.

Kajmak—Turkey and Jugoslavia (Serbia). Known as "Turkish butter." A soft, creamy cheese from ewe's milk.

Kashkaval—Roumania (also Kaskaval and Caskcaval—Greece). Popular all over the Balkans. Needn't concern you much.

Kasseri—Greece. A rather hard, Cheddar-like cheese.

King Christian IX—Denmark. A mild Samsoe with caraway.

Kloster—Germany. Soft, ripe, finger-shaped. Originally made by the monks.

Kopanisti—Greece. A blue cheese—sharp and peppery.

Kuminost—Scandinavia. A spiced cheese—various types. With caraway and cumin.

Kümmelkäse—Germany and U.S.A. A cheese to nibble while drinking anything from beer to kümmel.

Laguiole—France (also Guiole and Fourme de Laguiolle). A hard cheese made near Bordeaux. Resembles Cantal. Mostly used in cookery in place of Gruyère.

Lancashire—Great Britain. A popular cheese in England, especially for cooking and melting. White, sharp, crumbly with more flavor than Cheddar.

Langres—France. A very ancient cheese from the Haute-Marne. Semisoft; semihard—not unlike a Livarot or Maroilles.

Leather—Germany (also Leder). This is the pride of the Holstein cattle; made in Schleswig-Holstein, so it's half German and half Danish.

Leicester—Great Britain. One of England's best. Resembles Cheddar but more highly colored—orange to red.

Leyden—Holland (also Leyde). A semisoft, tangy cheese—made so by the inclusion of caraway and cuminseed.

Liederkranz—U.S.A. This is a trademarked cheese, made in Ohio, and is America's answer to Limburger. It is mild, spreads nicely, and many consider it our greatest contribution to the cheese world.

Limburger—Germany (also Belgium). Some call it semisoft; some call it semihard. (Is a bottle half full or half empty?) It has long been maligned because of its rather strong odor.

Liptauer—Hungary. It's hard to say whether this is a cheese or a "dip"! It's a very soft, sharp, pickled sort of cheese, liberally endowed with capers, anchovies, paprika, and sometimes pimiento.

Livarot—France. This is one of France's best known cheeses. It comes from Calvados in Normandy. It is strong and comes distinctively banded in reeds and leaves. A he-man cheese.

Lodigiano—Italy (also Lombardo). One of those hard *grano* cheeses used for grating.

Lüneberg—Austria. I've never had it, but it is popular in this part of the world. Has characteristics, they say, of both Emmentaler and Limburger. Quite a combo!

Maconnais—France. A goat's milk cheese presented in little squares.

Maile—U.S.S.R. (also Maile Peuer). Crumbly, mild—from ewe's milk from the Crimea. You won't find it in every supermarket!

Mainauer—Germany (also Radolfzeller). A cheese from Lake Constance—between a Münster and a cream cheese.

Mainzer Hand—Germany. From naturally soured milk. Often presented in jars.

Manchego—Spain. A very rich cheese from ewe's milk.

Manteca—Italy (also Manteche). This is a tricky fellow. Butter is sealed within the cheese and somehow remains fresh for long periods. You spread cheese and butter at the same time.

Maroilles—France (also Marolles). A soft cow's milk cheese, made in various parts of Northern France. Popular and available. A little like Pont l'Évêque.

Mascapone—Italy (also Mascherpone). A very soft, delicious cream cheese from Lombardy.

Milano—Italy (also Stracchino di Milano, Fresco, Quardo). A soft cheese resembling Bel Paese.

Mimolette—France. A mild cheese resembling Edam and looking like it, too.

Minnesota Blue—U.S.A. An American attempt to copy Roquefort—not very successfully.

57

Mondseer-Schachtelkäse—Austria (also Mondseer). A Münster-Limburger type cross.

Monsieur—France (also Monsieur Fromage). A soft paste cheese. Emulates a Camembert, and very successfully.

Montasio—Italy (also Austria). Both for table use and cooking, not unlike Fontina.

Monterey—U.S.A. (also Monterey Jack and Jack, which see). A West Coast Cheddar from pasteurized milk. Can be great —or horrid.

Mozzarella—Italy. From down Naples way. Once made from buffalo milk! Now, there are more cows than buffaloes. Eaten when very fresh. Copied all over the U.S.

Münster—France. This famous cheese is made in the Vosges Mountains of Alsace, so near Germany that it is sometimes mistakenly called a German cheese. Semihard, somewhat akin to Pont l'Évêque. Both plain and with caraway. Widely imitated—sometimes badly, sometimes well.

Mysost—Norway (also made in Sweden and Denmark). Similar to Gjetost. National cheese of Norway. Very widely copied, not always successfully.

Neufchâtel—France. Soft, mild cheese, eaten fresh or cured. Very popular. Made in the U.S.A. from pasteurized milk.

Nieheimer—Germany. Made from sour milk in Prussia. Contains beer—ripened with hops.

Noekkelost—Norway. A cheese spiced with cumin, caraway, and sometimes cloves.

Nostrale—Italy. Comes in both hard and soft versions.

Oka—Canada. Medium soft—made by the Trappist monks in Canada from a secret formula originating in France.

Olivet—France. Some say cow and some say sheep. Comes in three types: 1. fresh, white; 2. blue, half ripened; 3. ripened in ashes.

Padano—Italy. A hard grating cheese.

Parmesan—Italy (also Parmigiano and Parmigiano-Reggiano). Can be eaten as a table cheese when young but is usually aged (twelve to fourteen months) and hardened to be king of the graters. U.S. version is younger, milder.

Pecorino—Italy (also Pecorino Romano, Sardo). A strong cheese from goat's milk, ewe's milk, or cow's milk. The best is from Sardinia. Bears marks of the molding basket.

Pepato—Italy. If you like pepper, you'll like this one—hot as Hades.

Petit-Suisse—France. Small, cylindrical containers of unripened cheese—creamy, rich, perishable, delish.

Pfister—Switzerland. A junior Swiss.

Philadelphia Cream—U.S.A. A brand, but so famous for seventy-five years it deserves special mention. (Made in New York despite the name.)

Picodon—France. A goat cheese. Often comes in little pots.

Pineapple—U.S.A. Once a great favorite—with your grandpappy. Name is for shape, not flavor. Actually it's a polished Cheddar.

Pont l'Evêque—French. Well-known, semisoft cheese, ripened by a special mold that gives the cheese its special tang. Wonderful when just right.

Poona—U.S.A. This soft, delicate cheese is mentioned with a tear. It was the most delicious cheese I've ever tasted made in the U.S.A. (New York). I haven't seen it in years. I'm told it's no longer made.

Port-Salut—France (also Port-du-Salut and St.-Paulin). A semifirm cheese first made a century ago by Trappist monks in the abbey at Port-Salut. Today its fame has spread it to many other abbeys—and to factories as well. The lay Port-Salut is called St.-Paulin.

Process—The name given to the "process" of grinding up cheeses, mixing by heating and stirring, and adding an emulsifier. Sometimes acids, vinegar, water, or flavoring materials are also added. It may then be left alone or smoked (or smoke flavor may be added).

Process Cheese Food—dairy products such as cream, milk or whey are added.

Process Cheese Spreads—more moisture added so they are spreadable. Fruit, vegetables, meats, etc., may be added.

Provolone—Italy (also Provole and Provoletti). One of Italy's most famous cheeses. Pear-shaped, golden yellow, from mild to strong depending on age. Provolone hangs in every Italian food shop in the world. The U.S. version just isn't as good.

Queso Blanco—South America. This is a generic name given to the myriad of *quesos* (cheeses) made in Latin America. For the most part, the cheeses are made on farms or in small factories. The cheese is eaten fresh, within a few days of making. It may be pressed, in which case it lasts two weeks to two months.

Rabaçal—Portugal. A well-known Portuguese cheese—sheep or goat. Comes in small cylinders.

Raclette—Switzerland (also Valais Raclette). The name applies to a number of cheeses primarily used in the making of Raclettes: e.g., the cheese is heated and the semimelted surface is scraped off. (See Bagnes.)

Rayon—Switzerland (also Raper). This cheese is a hard "Swiss" type, made in Switzerland and sent, for some reason, to Turpin to ripen. It starts life as Rayon, ends as Raper.

Reblochon—France. This popular and delectable cheese is from the mountains of Savoie. It's a little like Port-Salut.

Reggiano—Italy. Refers to a Parmesan-like cheese first made in Reggio Emilia, Italy.

Ricotta—Italy. An unsalted cottage cheese used for fruit and cheesecake desserts. Much is now made in the U.S.A.

Rinnen—Poland. A sour-milk cheese, caraway added.

Robbiole—Italy (also Rabbiola, Crescenza). A soft, fast ripening, cream-type cheese.

Romadur—Germany (also Romadura). A soft cheese with the consistency of Liederkranz. Besides Germany, some is made and exported from Austria, Hungary, and Switzerland.

Romano—Italy (also Incanestrato). One of the very hard grating cheeses—much copied in the U.S.

Roquefort—France. One of the, if not *the,* most famous cheeses of the world. The original blue-veined cheese. Name and origin rigorously protected. Can be made only in and around the village of Roquefort in Aveyron, southeast France, and cured in the local caves. If you do right by Roquefort, you get a diploma; if you do wrong (substituting Blue, for instance), you'll end in the brig.

Runesten—Denmark (also Herrgårdsost—Sweden). Much like a Swiss. Now made extensively in the U.S.A.

Saaland Pfarr—Sweden (also Prestost). Here's one for the book! Made and washed with whiskey.

Saanen—Switzerland. A semihard and mellow "Swiss." Takes six to nine years to ripen. It then is so hard the Swiss say you could use the cheeses for trolley-car wheels. And so long-lasting, one will do for life.

Sage—England and U.S.A. The American version is a Cheddar, spiced with sage. In England, more of a cream cheese, flavored with sage and colored green.

Saint—France. There are all manner of minor "Saints," mostly goat, or *chèvres:* Sts. Agathon, Amand-Montrond, Benoit, Claude, St.-Cyr, Florentine, Flour, Gelay, Heray, Honoré, Hubert, Ivel, Laurent, Lizier, Nectaire, Reine, Réiny, Stephano.

St.-Marcellin—France. This "Saint" needs a special word, it's so good. A goat cheese, made the way Brie is made. Blue mold is cultivated on the surface but does not penetrate. Usually wrapped in leaves.

St.-Nectaire—France. Farm-made only, in small quantities. A gourmet cheese.

St.-Paulin—France. Synonymous with Port-Salut.

Salame—Italy. A soft cheese stuffed into skins (like a sausage)

—a packing used for many processed cheeses in the U.S.A. Also the name for a large Provolone, because of its sausage shape.

Samsö—Denmark (also Samsoe). Hard, white, sharp. Sometimes golden. Very popular in Denmark.

Sanen, Skring—Switzerland. Variants of Raclette. Not generally available here.

Sapsago—Switzerland. A very ancient, very hard grating cheese, pungent and greenish from the admixture of powdered wild clover leaves.

Sassenage—France (also Gex, Septmoncel). A blue mold cheese, strong. Cows, goats, and sheep all contribute to its making.

Scamorze—Italy. A hard cheese, mild, like a Provolone. Once made of buffalo's milk, now cow's and goat's. Made in pear shape and tied in twos to hang from the rafters.

Scanno—Italy. From ewe's milk. Black rind. Smoky flavor.

Schmierkäse—Germany. German cottage cheese.

Schwarzenberger—Czechoslovakia, Austria. Limburger-type.

Septmoncel—France (see Sassenage).

Serra da Estrella—Portugal. A popular soft-paste ewe's milk cheese. A good one.

Silesian—Poland. Also made in Germany in the same way as Hand Cheese. Emulated in the U.S.A.

Spalen—Switzerland. Very hard, very good, cow's milk cheese —sharp and nutty. Cured eighteen months to three years. Used for grating.

Spitzkäse—Germany. Limburger-like. Caraway seeded.

Steinbuscher—Germany (also Steinbuscher Käse). A rich cream cheese, yellow and spreadable.

Stilton—England. Without exception, England's finest. First made in Leicestershire, but its name is from Stilton in Huntingdonshire. A blue-mold cheese, rich, crumbly, mellow. Big mistakes are to scoop out bits with a spoon or to douse with Brandy. Cut off what you need and wrap the rest in a damp towel. The English like to push the Stilton (clockwise of course) round the table in small, handsome mahogany baskets with brass casters.

Stracchino—Italy (also Crescenza, Certoss). A rich goat cheese. Taleggio is the best known variety.

Sveciaost—Sweden. Popular in Sweden. Resembles Gouda.

Swiss—Switzerland. Made in dozens of countries. The genuine is Emmentaler, which see.

Taleggio—Italy. My favorite among the Italian cheeses. Soft, whole milk cheese—white, firm Stracchino texture, delicate, delicious.

Tamie—France (also Tamié). A look-alike for Port-Salut. Made by those monks again.

Teleme—Roumania, Bulgaria, Greece, Turkey. A sharp, pickled cheese, not unlike Feta and Briza.

Tillamook—U.S.A. Name given to Oregon's Cheddar pride.

Tilsiter—Germany, Norway, Denmark (also Tilsit, Ragnit). Rather like an American Brick or Port-Salut. Pleasant but not exciting.

Tome de Beaumont—France. A mild cow's milk cheese.

Tome de Savoie—France (also Tome de Raisin). A firm yellow paste cheese. Well liked—by me too.

Toscano—Italy (also Toscanello). Ewe's milk cheese not unlike Romano. Table cheese until it hardens.

Trappist—Jugoslavia, Hungary, Czechoslovakia. First made in a monastery in Bosnia. Now made all over Europe and even in Canada.

Travnik—Jugoslavia (also Arnautski Sir). Soft sheep and goat cheese, also popular in Albania, Turkey, and thereabouts.

Trouville—France. Soft, ripened cheese of the Pont l'Évêque family.

Tybo—Denmark. Rectangular—with or without caraway. Mild. Made for slicing.

Urda—Roumania. Creamy, soft, mild.

Uri—Switzerland. From the canton of that name. Hard, brittle, tangy.

Vacherin—Switzerland and France. Vacherin à la Main from Savoie is soft, like a Brie. Spreads easily. There is also a Swiss Vacherin and a Vacherin du Mont d'Or, and a Vacherin des Beauges—the last, almost extinct.

Valençay—France (also Levroux). A *chèvre* from Berry. Comes in pyramid shape. Popular.

Vendôme—France. A good, soft cheese, like Camembert. Sometimes ripened under ashes. The Parisians corner the market.

Veneto—Italy. Another one of those graters.

Warsawski—Poland. A hard, Cheddar-like cheese. Rare here.

Wensleydale—England. A hard, blue-veined cheese from Yorkshire, akin to Stilton.

Westphalia Sanermilch—Germany. A famous cheese, as well known as Westphalian ham. Butter, egg, caraway are added. A superlative "butter."

Wilstermarsch—Germany. Semihard, full cream, not unlike Tilsiter.

Wiltshire—England (also Truckles). Similar to Derby or Gloucester. Not often seen.

Yoghurt—Bulgaria. Made by using special cultures as starters, which give it its sharp flavor. Made in Mediterranean countries and also Canada. American yoghurt is less of a cheese, more of a coagulated milk.

Ziegel—Austria. A cow's milk cheese, made with added cream. Rich.

Ziger—Central Europe. Not a true cheese, but a whey product, an inexpensive albumin food, made in all countries of Central Europe—sometimes flavored with vinegar.

RECICPES

APPETIZERS
(and Lunch Dishes)

Carré au Fromage

(An appetizer)

(Serves 8)

1 package Boursault or Boursin
2 cups Port-Salut, St.-Paulin or Bonbel, in bits
1 cup bread or cracker crumbs
2 teaspoons cuminseed

Warm cheeses, blend well, and roll in crumbs. Shape into a 1½-inch-thick block. Sprinkle with cumin. Chill. Serve as an hors d'oeuvre with French bread.

Camembert Loaf

(An appetizer)

(Serves 4–6)
1 Camembert
¼ cup butter
2 tablespoons Cognac or Calvados
½ cup chopped, toasted almonds

Soften cheese and butter by leaving out of the refrigerator several hours. Mash butter and cheese together with the spirit to moisten. Form a ball. Roll in almonds. Refrigerate. Slice to serve.

Quiche Lorraine

(Serves 6–8)
1½ cups flour
½ teaspoon salt
¼ pound butter (soft)
2–3 tablespoons cold water
1 dozen strips bacon
4 eggs
1½ cups cream
Salt and pepper
Pinch nutmeg
Pinch sugar
1 cup grated real Swiss (or ¾ Swiss and ¼ Parmesan)

Work flour, salt, butter, and water together to make a ball.

Chill for an hour. Roll out thin and line 10″ pie plate or quiche tin. Put in refrigerator.

Cook the bacon (not too done). Crumble over piecrust.

Preheat oven to 400°. Break eggs into bowl. Add cream, salt and pepper, nutmeg, sugar. Mix well. Sprinkle the cheese over bacon. Pour in egg custard mixture. Bake in oven for 10 minutes. Reduce heat to 350° for about 25 minutes until pie is nicely browned. Let cool a minute before cutting.

Cheese Pie No. 1

(Serves about 6)

Crust: **1 package cream cheese blended with 3 ounces softened butter.** Add enough flour for a dough. Knead and refrigerate overnight.

Next day preheat oven to 375°; roll out dough on floured board, to make a crust in buttered pie plate.

Filling: Brush dough with melted butter or milk. Fill with **½ pound grated Switzerland Swiss,** mixed with a smidgen of pepper, salt, and nutmeg. Bake at 375° for 30 minutes or until nicely browned.

Cheese Pie No. 2

(Serves 6–8)

Crust: **1½ cups graham cracker crumbs**
2 tablespoons sugar
½ cup melted butter

Grease a 10″ pie pan. Mix crumbs, sugar, and butter. Press
    into sides and bottom of pan. Refrigerate.
Center: **1 pound cream cheese**
    ½ cup light cream
    ½ cup sugar
    2 eggs
    2 teaspoons vanilla
Preheat oven to 350°. Beat cheese well. Add cream. Beat. Add
    sugar. Beat. Add eggs. Beat. Add vanilla. Pour into shell.
    Bake 20 minutes.
    Before serving: **1 cup sour cream**
    1 tablespoon sugar
    ½ teaspoon vanilla
    Berries (fresh strawberries, blueberries,
        or raspberries)
Beat first 3 ingredients together. Smear over pie. Return to
    oven. Cook 5 minutes. Chill. Top with fresh berries.

Baked Cheese "Things"

(Makes 3 dozen cookies or strips)
1¼ cups butter (soft)
2 cups flour
2 cups grated cheese (Cheddar or similar)
Salt and pepper

Mix all ingredients, butter and flour first. Chill in refrigerator overnight.

Preheat oven to 375°. Roll out dough and cut into cookie sizes or strips. Put on cookie sheets. (If strips, curl into corkscrews.) Bake in oven until brown (about 15 minutes).

Pizza!

(Buy 'em if anyone in the neighborhood makes 'em—decently. Else, it's quite a deal.)
Dough: 1 package yeast dissolved in warm water
2 cups flour
1 teaspoon salt
3 tablespoons soft butter (or 2 tablespoons olive oil)

Mix all together and knead for 10 minutes. Make a ball. Put in a bowl. Cover tightly. Let stand 3 or 4 hours in a warm spot.
Paste: 3 medium onions—sliced
3 tablespoons olive oil
1½ cans tomato paste
½ teaspoon orégano
Salt
Crushed chili pepper (or ½ cup frozen green pepper)

2½ cups water

2 small cans anchovies, diced (or anchovy paste)

Fry onion in oil to yellow. Stir in paste. Add seasonings. Add water. Simmer slowly ½ hour. Anchovies go in at end.

Cheese: ¾ cup (freshly) grated Parmesan, Romano, Pecorino
—or any combination

Pizza: Now you're ready. Preheat oven to 400°. Get your pizza pan—12 inch or larger. Grease. Roll out dough about ¼ inch thick and line your tin. Rub with olive oil. Pour in paste. Sprinkle with cheese. Bake at 400° for 25 to 30 minutes, until golden brown and bubbly.

SOUPS

Cheese Soup

(Serve 6–8)

4 tablespoons butter

4 tablespoons flour

4 cups good chicken broth

3 cups grated sharp Cheddar (freshly grated is best)

2 cups milk

Salt and pepper

Dry Sherry to taste

(For an interesting variant—to ingredients add 4 cups chopped raw vegetables such as carrots, celery, onion, green pepper, cucumber, green beans.)

Melt butter in double boiler. (Add vegetables, if used, and cook slowly—about 10 minutes, adding a little butter if necessary.) Sprinkle with flour. Add broth. Cook until boiling and thickened. Add cheese and melt. Keep cooking. Add cold milk. Keep cooking over boiling water until very hot, and then some (about 15 minutes). Season to taste. When ready to serve, lace with 2 or 3 tablespoons of a decent Sherry.

Soupe du Jurade

(Serves 4)
4 cups cream of tomato soup
1 bouquet garni (parsley, bay leaf, 1 clove, dash allspice, dash saffron)
1 tablespoon olive oil
1 clove garlic, crushed
1 medium onion, chopped
3 tablespoons heavy cream
1 raw egg yolk
2 tablespoons grated Swiss or Gruyère

Put soup, bouquet, oil, garlic, and onion into a saucepan. Heat to boil. Remove bouquet. Mix cream and egg yolk. Pour on top of soup. Garnish with cheese.

EGGS

Scrambled, with Cheese

(Serves 4)
8 eggs
½ cup grated Münster (or Cheddar)

Salt and pepper
1 teaspoon chopped chives (freeze-dried will do)
3 tablespoons butter

Break eggs into a bowl. Beat together just enough to break the yolks. Add cheese, salt and pepper, and chives. Break butter into small bits and stir into the egg mixture. Turn into skillet and cook, constantly stirring, until eggs are consistency you like.

Omelet, with Cheese

(Serves 2)
5 eggs
1 teaspoon Worcestershire sauce
3 tablespoons butter
½ cup grated Cheddar (or grated Swiss)—or ¼ cup Parmesan—it's stronger

Break eggs into bowl and stir just enough to break yolks. Stir in Worcestershire.

Put butter into skillet. Heat skillet to point where butter begins to brown. Pour egg mix into pan and begin to shake hard, back and forth, at the same time lifting omelet edges to let soft egg run under. When top is still moist, shake in the cheese. Cook a moment longer. Fold over in half, and slide out onto heated platter.

PASTA
(All pasta—spaghetti, macaroni, ravioli, cappelletti, and a thousand more—tastes better with a good shake of cheese.)

Fettuccine all'Alfredo

(This, probably the most famous pasta recipe in the world—even if you *don't* toss it with Alfredo's celebrated gold fork!).
(Serves 8)
1 pound fettuccine (bought'n noodles will have to do if you're not of a mind to roll your own!)
½ pound sweet butter
1½ cups freshly grated Parmesan
½ cup heavy cream (optional)
Cook noodles in salted boiling water until tender but firm (*al dente*). Drain. Place *at once* in large serving dish and add remaining ingredients, half at a time. Toss and toss while noodles are still very hot, to melt butter and cheese.

76

Lasagne

(Serves 6–8)
1 pound wide noodles
Salt and pepper
1½ cups tomato sauce (the thick kind)
½ pound Ricotta (cottage cheese will do)
1 pound Mozzarella (or Cheddar)
¼ pound grated cheese (Parmesan or Romano or both)

Preheat oven 375°. Cook noodles by the recipe on the box until *al dente* (not soft, not hard). Season with salt and pepper. In a baking dish, pour ½ cup tomato sauce, cover with ¼ of the noodles, sprinkle with ⅓ of each of the 3 cheeses. Keep on layering, 3 times. End with sauce and the grated cheese on top. Bake for 15 minutes. Shake more cheese on as you serve.

ACCOMPANIMENTS
(to the Main Course)

Risotto alla Milanese

(You *can* make this famous dish without marrow; you could also make ham and eggs without ham!)
(Serves 4–6)
Marrow bones (or marrow)—enough to make 3–4 tablespoons marrow when melted
1 medium onion, chopped
1½ cups rice (preferably regular long-cook)
3 cups chicken broth (or beef stock or bouillon)
A pinch of saffron (optional)

2 tablespoons butter
5 tablespoons freshly grated Parmesan

First, take marrow from bones and melt. Sauté onion in marrow. Add rice and coat well. In another pot, heat broth. Add soup cup by cup, leaving time in between for absorption by the rice. (Add saffron—moistened a little—if you're going to use it.) When rice is softened and not too liquid, add butter and cheese. Stir well, cook a bit to melt cheese. Serve very hot.

Potatoes Anna with Cheese

(This is simply the famous "Anna" potatoes with cheese added.)
(Serves 4)
2 cups sliced potatoes (raw rather than cooked; if cooked reduce cooking time)
¾ cup grated sharp Cheddar
Dabs of butter
½ cup milk
1 egg, beaten
3 tablespoons butter
Salt and pepper
¼ cup grated Parmesan

Preheat oven to 350°. In a buttered baking dish, layer potatoes, cheese, dabs of butter. Keep on until all are used up. Stir milk, egg, butter, salt and pepper—pour over. Top with Parmesan. Bake for an hour or a bit more. Should be nice and brown on top.

Vegetables au Gratin or Mornay

Most of the following vegetables take similar preparation; e.g., in a Mornay sauce (which see).

Asparagus—Cook until nearly soft. Pour over a Mornay sauce. Sprinkle with bread crumbs. Dot with butter. Bake in hot oven until crumbs brown.

Broccoli—Sauté rosettes of broccoli in hot butter. Sprinkle with Parmesan or Romano cheese.

Celery—Clean, scrape, and cut celery into 1-inch chunks. Cook in salt water (or stock) 20 minutes or until soft. Drain. Cover with Mornay sauce. Put in scallop shells. Sprinkle with Parmesan. Brown quickly under broiler.

Eggplant—Wash and cut 1 eggplant into ½-inch slices. Cover with hot water. Let stand 5 minutes. Chop 6 tomatoes and put into skillet with 2 tablespoons olive oil, 1 tablespoon tomato paste, salt. Simmer, uncovered, 30 minutes.

Drain and dry eggplant. Sauté in hot olive oil, 3 minutes a side. Sprinkle salt and pepper.

Mix 2 cups bread crumbs, ½ cup grated Parmesan, 1 tablespoon chopped parsley, 2 cloves garlic, finely chopped. Blend.

In a casserole, place a layer of eggplant, a layer of crumbs, and a layer of tomato sauce. Alternate layering. Top with slices of Mozzarella cheese. Bake at 375° for 10 minutes.

Mushrooms—Marinate 1 pound sliced mushrooms in ½ cup olive oil, and 1 tablespoon each grated onion, chopped shallots, chives, parsley, and chervil. Add pulp of 1 garlic kernel, mashed, pinches tarragon, thyme, salt and pepper,

and 3 tablespoons tarragon vinegar. Stand 2 hours or more. Drain.

Melt ⅓ cup butter. Sauté slices 10 minutes. Put into baking dish. Sprinkle top with bread crumbs mixed with ½ cup grated Parmesan. Brown under broiler.

Spinach—Wash and dry 2 pounds spinach. Chop ½ pound mushrooms quite fine and cook 4 or 5 minutes in butter. Drain. Cover with Mornay sauce.

In baking dish, layer mushrooms and spinach. On top pour last of Mornay. Sprinkle with Parmesan or Cheddar and bread crumbs. Brown under broiler.

Cheese Ramekins

(Makes about 4—depending upon size of ramekins)

Dough: 2½ ounces margarine (½ bar plus 1 tablespoon)
  4 ounces flour
  Dash each salt and sugar
  ¼ cup lukewarm water

Filling: 1 egg
  1 ounce flour
  ¼ cup milk
  ¼ cup heavy cream
  Dash of salt, pepper, nutmeg
  4 ounces grated natural Gruyère
  ¼ cup finely diced smoked or boiled ham
  2 ounces Switzerland Swiss cheese, cut into small cubes

Dough: Cut margarine into flour and mix by hand until fairly smooth and compact. Dissolve salt and sugar in lukewarm water. Mix water with dough and let rest overnight in refrigerator. Roll out on board when ready to use. Preheat oven to 325°.

Filling: In blender, mix egg and flour, add milk, heavy cream, seasonings and the grated Gruyère cheese. Line individual buttered ramekin forms with dough. Add chopped ham. Pour in filling (½ full). Place cubes of Switzerland Swiss on top. Bake at 325° until golden brown, about 15 minutes.

Croque Monsieur

(For 1 sandwich)
1 heaping tablespoon freshly grated Swiss cheese
1 tablespoon heavy cream
2 slices bread
1 slice ham
1 egg, beaten
Butter for frying

Make a paste of cheese and cream. Smear on both pieces of bread. Put ham on one slice and make sandwich. Dip outsides of bread into egg and fry in butter until just browning. (Nice Nellies cut off crusts of bread.)

Croque Madame

Substitute white meat of chicken for ham, or if you're really hungry, use both!

Welsh "Rabbit"

(Or "Rarebit." The argument continues as to which is correct. The argument also continues as to how to make it. I find this recipe good.)
(Serves 3)

1 tablespoon butter

8 ounces finely ground aged Cheddar (or Cheshire)

4 tablespoons stale beer or ale (open the beer well ahead, or use leftover from yesterday—stir out the bubbles as much as possible)

2 teaspoons dry mustard

2 teaspoons Worcestershire sauce

Salt and pepper

1 or 2 egg yolks

Put butter and cheese in saucepan with the beer and cook until melted. Stir in mustard, Worcestershire, and salt and pepper to taste. Keep stirring all the while until mixture thickens. Remove from fire. Beat in egg yolk or yolks. Pour over toast points.

Golden Buck

Simply put poached eggs on top of the individual rarebits—or a strip or two of bacon—or both.

Rum Tum Tiddy
(Also Scotch Woodcock)

1 onion, minced

1 tablespoon butter

Salt and pepper

2 cups canned tomatoes
1 tablespoon sugar
3 cups grated Cheddar
1 egg, slightly beaten

Fry onions in butter—season and add to tomatoes and sugar. Heat just to boil. Add cheese to melt. Stir in egg. A little Sherry at end won't hurt. 2 tablespoons anchovy paste and slices of hard-cooked egg make this a Scotch Woodcock.

The plain, basic Welsh Rabbit may be used as a sauce with high marks. Just pour it over grilled sardines, broiled roes, cooked seafood, chipped beef, grilled tomatoes, boiled onions, sautéed mushrooms, and the like—or be the first on your avenue to invent other Rabbits.

FONDUES

Fondue

(Here's another one of those recipe hassles that bring out the worst in everyone!)

(Serves 4–6)

1 clove garlic

1½ cups dry white wine (Swiss Neufchâtel or Fendant is traditional, but a nice Alsatian, German, or U. S. Riesling will do nicely)

1 pound real Swiss (Emmentaler or Switzerland Swiss), coarsely grated (or ½ pound Swiss and ½ pound Gruyère); 2 tablespoons grated Sapsago is a worthy addition

1 tablespoon cornstarch (or flour)—optional

3 tablespoons Kirsch (Cognac or Calvados will do in a pinch, so will a good jigger of Bourbon)
Dash nutmeg
Salt and pepper
Loaf French bread cut into bite-size cubes

Rub your casserole, earthenware pot, or whatever with garlic. Discard. Pour in wine. Heat well but do not boil. Add cheese, handful by handful, waiting for each batch to melt. Moisten cornstarch with Kirsch. Add to cheese mixture. Stir and continue cooking until just ready to boil. Add nutmeg, salt and pepper. Remove from fire. Keep warm over alcohol or Sterno heat. If too thick, thin with wine. Spear a piece of bread. Swish around in bowl to coat. Everyone takes turns. If bread comes off tines of fork, you must kiss the person to your right, assuming he or she is of the appropriate sex!

Fonduta alla Piedmontese

(This is an Italian version of fondue and a great one. Barbetta's Restaurant in New York specializes in it in season with fresh truffles.)

(Serves 4)

1 pound imported Fontina, diced
Milk to cover
4 tablespoons butter
5 egg yolks
Salt and pepper
4 white truffles (yes, I know—but with no truffles, it's no fonduta! Canned ones are available)
Bread chunks

Cover cheese with the milk and soak overnight. Put in pot over heat and melt cheese. Add butter, yolks, salt and pepper, stirring constantly. Place in fondue dish to keep warm. Add truffles. Serve with usual bread chunks.

Cheese Fondue à la Savoie
(The French version)

(Serves 4)

½ cup white wine
1 clove garlic, chopped
4 eggs
¼ cup melted butter
½ pound Gruyère, grated
Salt and pepper
Bread chunks

Cook wine and garlic. Reduce to half. Beat eggs, butter and cheese together. Season. Add to wine mixture. Cook until thick. Serve with bread chunks.

Variations—Use Vacherin cheese in place of Swiss or Gruyère, or Roquefort or Cheddar.

A couple of fresh tomatoes, skinned and chopped, with a little basil, are nice, in the recipe (or use ketchup and tomato soup).

A few chopped chives or shallots make a tasty addition.

Raclette

This isn't exactly a fondue; it's simply a way to eat melted cheese. It came from Valais, a canton of Switzerland. There, they place a hunk of Raclette cheese (*Bagnes* or *Conches*) in front of the open fire. As the surface melts, it is scraped off onto boiled potatoes or French bread. Help yourself. If a fireplace just doesn't happen to be handy, use a hibachi, an electric saucepan, or electric bake oven—or do it outside, over the open coals. Beer, or a light Swiss L'Aigle wine, would be lovely with this. Also a sliced ham, if the Raclette is the entire meal.

Fondues with Meat, etc., and Sauces

There are dozens of fondues—with beef, veal, chicken, fish, shrimp, even chocolate, etc., served with sauces—but neither the recipes nor the sauces call for cheese, for the most part, so

they have no real place in the confines of this already tight
little book. Sorry!

MAIN COURSES

Cheese Soufflé

(There are as many recipes for this as there are copper pots
on the S.S. *France*. This one will do pretty well.)
(Serves 4–6)
1 cup milk
Bay leaf
1 clove garlic, slivered
Salt and pepper
3 tablespoons butter
3 tablespoons flour
1 teaspoon dry mustard
1 cup grated cheese (Cheddar alone will do but ⅔ Cheddar and
 ⅓ Parmesan is better, or ⅓ each of Cheddar, Parmesan, and
 Swiss)
3 egg yolks, beaten
5 egg whites, whipped to stiffness
Butter to grease soufflé dish
Paprika to garnish
Preheat oven to 375°. Bring milk, bay leaf, garlic, salt and
pepper to boil. Take off heat. Cover. Let stand 5 minutes. In
another pot, melt butter. Stir in flour. Add mustard. Strain in
milk mixture. Bring to boil. Add cheese and stir well as it
melts. Off fire, stir in beaten egg yolks. Cool. Fold in egg whites
gently and not thoroughly. Pour into buttered soufflé dish. Add

88

garnish. Bake 30 to 40 minutes, until nicely risen. A mustard sauce goes nicely.

With the basic soufflé, you can try any number of variations:
Add:

1. A cup of finely chopped spinach and 1 tablespoon chopped onion, sautéed in butter and whipped until light before adding.

2. Tomato juice in place of milk.

3. Cup of mushroom soup and 2 tablespoons chopped, cooked bacon in place of milk.

Coquilles St. Jacques
(Mornay)

(Serves 6)
1 pound bay scallops (or cut-up sea scallops if you must)
Juice ½ lemon
½ pound fresh mushrooms, sautéed in 3 tablespoons butter
1 cup dry Vermouth (or 1½ cups dry white wine)
1 tablespoon chopped shallots

¼ cup water
2 tablespoons butter
1½ tablespoons flour
2 egg yolks
Salt and pepper
½ cup grated cheese (Cheddar or Swiss)

Squirt scallops with lemon. Sauté mushrooms. Cook scallops in Vermouth, shallots, and water, no more than 3 or 4 minutes (overcooking toughens). Add sautéed mushrooms. Cook another 2 minutes. Drain and reserve liquid.

In another pot, melt butter, add flour, add 1¼ cups wine sauce from scallops. Cook until thick. Stir in egg yolks, salt and pepper. Pour sauce over scallops. Fill scallop shells or ovenproof ramekins. Sprinkle with cheese and brown under grill.

Chicken with Tarragon and Cheese

(A particularly good *poulet* recipe.)
(Serves 6)
3 large chicken breasts, halved
¾ cup milk
Salt and pepper
1 cup grated Parmesan
8 ounces sweet butter
3 tablespoons shallots, chopped very fine (or onion, if you must)
¾ pint heavy cream
3 ounces dry Sherry
2 teaspoons dried tarragon

Skin breasts. Dip in milk. Salt and pepper. Dredge in cheese.

Sauté in ½ of the butter—8 minutes a side over medium heat. Remove pieces and keep warm. In same pan, put in last of the butter, and sauté the shallots, scraping bits from pan. Cook 5 or 6 minutes. Lower heat, add cream, Sherry, and tarragon and cook until mixture thickens. Return breasts to sauce. Coat well. Heat and Serve.

Veal Parmigiana

(Serves 4–6)
6 veal cutlets, pounded (by you or the butcher) until very thin
2 eggs, beaten
¾ cup bread crumbs
Salt and pepper
4 tablespoons grated Parmesan
2 tablespoons olive oil
1 cup tomato sauce
6 slices Mozzarella

Dip veal pieces in egg. Mix crumbs, salt and pepper, and 3 tablespoons cheese. Coat slices liberally. Sauté in hot oil quickly, a few minutes per side until golden. Put in baking pan. Pour tomato sauce over. Top with cheese slices. Sprinkle with remaining Parmesan cheese. Bake 10–15 minutes at 375° until cheese melts and browns.

Sauce Mornay

(Makes about 1½ cups)

Again, there are dozens of recipes. For the classic cheese sauce, first make a béchamel sauce with 2 tablespoons each of butter and flour, a cup of milk, and a tablespoon of finely diced onion. When thick and hot, add ½ cup dry white wine. Boil to reduce. Stir in 2 tablespoons grated Cheddar and 1 tablespoon grated Parmesan (just one cheese will do). Salt and pepper to season. For a lighter sauce, stir in a couple of tablespoons of whipped cream before using or serving.

Pesto Genovese

This is *the* sauce for pasta—the one and only *professional* one. (Traditionally made in mortar and pestle; today use the blender.)

(Makes about 1½ cups)

½ cup olive oil

2 cloves garlic, slivered

1 cup fresh basil or 2 teaspoons dried

¼ cup grated Sardo cheese

¼ cup grated Parmesan (if no Sardo, ½ cup Parmesan)

¼ cup pine nuts (pignolias) or ¼ cup walnuts

½ teaspoon salt

Put into blender. Whirr-rr! Will freeze for future use.

Roquefort Dressing

(Makes about 2 cups)
1 cup Roquefort (no other or you'll be in the clink!)
⅔ cup salad (or olive) oil
1 tablespoon Worcestershire sauce
1 tablespoon lemon juice
2 tablespoons wine (or tarragon) vinegar
½ clove garlic, minced

Mash cheese with some of the oil. Add everything else. Shake or beat until creamy.

Cream Cheese Dressing

(Makes about 1 cup)

Mix 1 package (½ cup) cream cheese with ½ teaspoon dry mustard, 1 teaspoon tarragon. Gradually beat in 4 tablespoons olive oil, 1 tablespoon lemon juice, salt and pepper.

DESSERTS

Coeur à la Crème

(Serves 6)
2 cups cottage cheese
2 cups cream cheese (2 blocks)
2 cups heavy cream
½ cup light cream
2 cups thawed frozen strawberries

Combine the cheeses well and force through fine sieve. Beat well. Whip heavy cream until stiff and stir in cheese mixture. For tradition's sake, use a heart-shaped mold. Line with cheesecloth. Turn the cheese mix in. Chill overnight. When ready to serve, unmold, pour a little light cream over and surround with strawberries.

Cheese Blintzes

(Allow 3 or 4 pancakes per person. This recipe makes about 12 to 15.)

Pancakes: **6 eggs, beaten**
⅛ teaspoon salt
4 tablespoons flour
2 tablespoons ice cold water

Beat eggs and salt. Mix flour and water and half the beaten egg. Pour into the rest of the egg.

Now, using a 6-inch heavy skillet or crêpe pan, heat until a speck of butter will sizzle. Grease pan with a *little* butter. Pour in enough batter to make a very thin coating. As soon as pancake bubbles, invert pan over a platter so uncooked side of pancake is down. Make all pancakes the same way.

Filling: (**There are dozens, of course—fruit, meat, etc.—but this filling is cheese.**)
1½ pounds farmer or dry cottage cheese
1 beaten egg
Salt and pepper

Preheat oven to 375°. Mix all ingredients well. Place a tablespoon in each pancake. Fold over securely. Bake in oven until blintz is browning.

Cheesecake

(This makes a cake big enough for a dozen.)

Crust: **1 cup flour**
¼ cup sugar
1 teaspoon grated lemon rind
¼ teaspoon vanilla
¼ cup melted butter
1 egg yolk

Mix flour, sugar, lemon rind, vanilla. Make a hollow and put in butter and egg yolk. Work together into a ball. Chill an hour or overnight.

Preheat oven to 400°. Roll out dough thinly, and line cake pan. Bake crust for 15 minutes—until golden brown.

Filling: 2½ pounds cream cheese
1¾ cups sugar
3 tablespoons flour
1½ teaspoons grated lemon rind
1½ teaspoons grated orange rind
¼ teaspoon vanilla
5 eggs
2 extra egg yolks
¼ cup heavy cream

Combine first 6 ingredients (up to eggs) in order given. Give them a good whirr-rr in an electric mixer (several loads). Add eggs and egg yolks, one at a time, whirring lightly. Stir in cream at the end. Pour into baked crust and chill.

Pineapple Cheesecake

2½ pounds pot cheese
¼ pound sweet butter, melted
5 eggs
1½ cups sugar
2 cups milk
⅓ cup flour
1½ teaspoons vanilla extract
2 cups graham cracker crumbs (or crush graham crackers)
2 tablespoons butter
Small can crushed pineapple, drained

Preheat oven to 350°. Mix everything except last 3 ingredients. Grease a deep Pyrex pan. Mix crumbs and butter.

Spread over pan and press down. Bake 5 or 6 minutes. Pour in pineapple evenly. Pour in the cheese mix and spread evenly. Bake about 1 hour at 350°. Let stand.

Cheese-Matzo Kugel

(Serves 4)
6 eggs
⅔ cup milk
3 matzos
Salt and pepper
8 tablespoons butter
½ pound Münster, thinly sliced (or other mild cheese)
3 tablespoons sugar
1⅓ cups sour cream

Beat eggs with milk and break matzos into this (very small pieces). Season—salt and pepper. Leave 10 or 15 minutes.

Melt part of the butter in a large skillet. Pour in half the mixture. Cook until bottom is set. Cover top with ½ the cheese slices. When beginning to melt, fold pancake over and cook a minute or so more. Turn and cook other side. Place in warm platter. Spread with ½ the remaining butter, sugar and dollops of cream. Now do the same to the other half, and make another pancake. Serve half to a person.

Fruit & Cheese
(The Marriage Made in Heaven)

Any fruit will do as long as it's good quality and ripe (citrus fruits don't do quite as well). Serve flavorful cheeses with flavorful fruits, mild cheeses with delicate fruits.

Viz:

Peaches, strawberries, raspberries, mango—with Brie.
Pears (Comice, Anjou)—with Roquefort or Bleu.
    (Bartlett, papaya)—with Camembert.
Apples, apricots—with Cheddar.
Table Grapes—with Danish mild cheeses or Bel Paese.

CODICIL MORNAY

I started this small book with the verbal graffito: "Cheese it!"

We have discussed the history of cheese, the making of cheese, the buying of cheese, the storing of cheese, the serving of cheese. We have then gone into a cheese lexicon—cheeses from A to Zed—some of which you know, some of which you've heard, and some of which you've never heard. Even this list isn't complete, for cheeses are a many-timey thing. Don't feel bad if you can't try them all—or even *find* half of them in the shop. But do keep trying some new ones and discovering new delights. Cheddar may be good, Brie may be super, even some process cheese you've found may be tasty, but variety is the spice of cheese. Enjoy it! Join the "new cheese a day" club—or at least, every *other* day.

Try some of the cheese recipes. Nothing cooks as quickly, smells so good, or is more delectable as a first, middle, or last course.

Perhaps, if you do some of these things, you'll become the turophile that most of us are but don't realize.

In other words don't say "cheese" and smile, but smile and say "cheese."

INDEX